FROM THE WILDERNESS

Poems by

ALASDAIR MACLEAN

LONDON . VICTOR GOLLANCZ LTD . 1973

ISBN 0 575 01703 1

821
MᶜLE

PRINTED IN GREAT BRITAIN
BY EBENEZER BAYLIS AND SON LIMITED
THE TRINITY PRESS, WORCESTER, AND LONDON

FOR MY PARENTS

ACKNOWLEDGEMENTS

Some of the poems in this volume have appeared or are about to appear in the following outlets, though not always in the same form or under the same title: *The Critical Quarterly, Lines, The Listener, Poetry Introduction Two, Poetry Review, The Scotsman, Scottish International, Transatlantic Review* and various anthologies and various European and American magazines. Acknowledgements are also due to BBC Radio Three and Four and BBC Television. Finally, I would like to offer my grateful thanks to the Scottish Arts Council whose 1971 award of a bursary enabled me to complete this book.

FROM THE WILDERNESS

CONTENTS

TO THE READER

I am not bondsman to your least shout,
nor friend; perhaps, if I could choose, more foe.
Only it is my trade to lead you carefully
astray in lands where no mapmakers go.

It will not serve to whistle then nor pray
nor quote authority nor put on speed.
What keeps you upright in your shoes, your needle
to the poem's north, is a sort of greed.

I leave the foothills of the images
and climb. What I pursue's not means but ends.
You may come, if you've a mind to travelling.
Meet me at the point where the language bends.

AT THE PEATS

In March we start our harvesting.
We dig ourselves down out of sight
in a peat bog,
continuing perhaps all summer
when the weather lets us,
till the job is done.
My father and myself.
We work in harmony at first,
he cutting and I spreading,
backwards and forwards,
up and down,
the rhythm of the cradle.
Then in May the sun comes north,
thawing out the silence,
and the tourists sprout.
They prod us with their cameras,
making us aware of what we do,
and once we appeared in the *Scottish Field*
in a photograph so clear
you could count the midges.
Highland peasants cutting peat.
The abundance of free fuel
is an important factor in the crofting economy.
One of my father's rare grim smiles,
like a lull in the east wind,
broke out when I read that to him.

STONE

I

A long peninsula of solid rock,
upholstered every year in threadbare green.
Stones everywhere, ambiguous and burgeoning.
In Sanna ramparts of them
march around our crofts
but whether to keep cattle out or other stones
no man can say.
And at Kilchoan there were three houses
cropped from one field.
That was when I was a boy.
The masons left the pebbles
and there's a castle now, waiting to be harvested.
God was short of earth when He made Ardnamurchan.

II

Hugh Macdonald, crofter, of Glendryan
and Hector Henderson, crofter, of Sanna
fought to the death in a field near here
in 1868, in a ring marked by stones.
They began at dawn and it was early evening
when they finished. Hugh Macdonald won.
He battered his opponent to the ground
then sat astride his chest to kill him.
He punched full weight at the head below,
again and again and again and again,
driving down through bone and brain
till there was nothing left to punch at.

11

It was as if a headless body lay there.
After it was over the winner was accused
by Alan Henderson, shoemaker, of this parish
of having pebbles hidden in his hands.
He was seized by the Sanna crofters and examined.
His fists, they found, had locked shut; fists no more
but lumps of stone. The parish record says
they had to break his fingers to get them open.

III

'From stone you came,' said the preacher, 'and to stone
you shall return. Stone you must be all your days.
Come, let me chisel you!' That was John MacIan,
Doctor of Divinity, ordained minister of this parish
in 1800, dismissed his post within a year.
'The shortest catechism,' he said also, 'is a glimpse
of your own cattle ripening on your own hill.'
And, 'Last spring you burned Black Margaret
as a witch. Who am I to forgive you?'
To the gentry in the laird's pew one Sunday
he handed slivers of stone, saying they were pieces
of the true cross. He emptied churches for miles around
and overflowed his own. Burgess and beggar stood
knee-deep in the surrounding fields to hear him
and be heard. 'Solve me and save you,' he said.
He preached his first and last Easter sermon
from his own cutty stool and was adjudged heterodox
at the next Session. What happened to him after,
God knows. But sometimes in the late evening,
when an older ministry is at work, I lean
across the churchyard wall to watch the night
come into its own. My neighbours house themselves

for fear of the unruly dead; my blood,
that all day long would not take 'no'
for an answer, inches towards my heart
and the all-forgiving darkness rises stone
by stone past door and window, tower and bell,
till church and Ardnamurchan are one.
If I say he lives, he lives. His rule of thumb
for preaching is the one I use to write:
'a plain statement of the marvellous
and a marvellous statement of the plain.'

IV

My grandfather, when he was old,
would sit for hours above the village,
poised on the hillside like a rock.
If you crept up behind him you could hear
him muttering, a curse and a curse and a curse.
He dredged the decades and there was no one
from the carpenter who made his cradle onwards
he didn't curl his tongue around,
no incident since his incidents began
he couldn't remould nearer to his heart's desire.
It was an education to sit and listen—
the time someone did this . . . did that . . .
the time . . . the time . . . the time—
over and over again, obsessively, adoringly,
he told his wounds. Longevity in the making.
His soft coevals fell away, destroyed by love,
and from their funerals he walked home clinking.
Seventy, eighty, ninety upwards.
He was still muttering when he took to bed
and there was never the least crack in him.

V

Before there was a churchyard on soft ground
at Kilchoan, or carts to carry bodies to it,
there were folk at Sanna. When they died
their followers could find no earth with depth
for even a shallow grave. They had a choice
between bog and beach and who'd want the bog,
to lie suspended through the centuries,
with every scar still ready for the probe
and every wrinkle signalling. It's politic
to shed flesh while the shedding's good
and hope for a better fit next time.
They chose the beach and there they are today
under the short turf. No stone within a mile of them,
only the weight of time and the wind's slow curiosity.
I could wish my own bones, when I hand them back,
so soft a bed, so sweet and cool a resurrection.

SOME RULES FOR VISITING A DESERTED HOUSE

Look behind the door for letters.
Any that you find read sympathetically.
If there are bills decide to pay them.

Don't worry about rats.
If any did live here
they will have left.
Too much competition now.

As for ghosts
they will not be those of popular fiction
but intermingled and continuous with the air.
You will be all right if you don't stay too long
or breathe too deeply.

Watch out for the loose section of carpet
when going up the stair.
It will be in a different place
when you come down.

Avoid the mirror on the landing.
It will be thirsty.

Check the bedroom.
If there is only one impression on the pillow
make another.
If there are two erase one.

15

Check the bathroom.
If something looks like rust in the bathtub
wet it.
Touch it to see if it feels sticky.

In the loft, under the eaves,
will be the skeletons of small trapped birds.
You may examine them
but be sure to put them back.
They are trophies.

If, in spite of everything,
you find the outside door jammed shut
when you are ready to depart
don't bother going to the windows.
They also will have been attended to.
Sit down and wait.
Try not to think about the small birds.

DEVIL MASK FROM THE WEST HIGHLANDS

This morning when I walked along the beach
I came across a fishing float of black plastic
that had been pounded by the sea to bits.
One bit was triangular,
with a fringe of green weed for hair,
with two holes for eyes
where the rope had been,
with smears of tar for nose and mouth.
It lay on the sand and grinned up at me.

When I was a child here
there was a whole lot of sin going on.
More than there is now.
It was all the work of the Devil.
He was everywhere.
He was in your eyes and in your mouth.
He visited your bed at night.
If you left a hole open he would enter in.
Even a pore.
You had to scrunch yourself up very tight.

On Sundays he came for sure.
You were pressed into your good suit
and sent to meet him.
The minister pounded his lectern of driftwood.
He went bang, bang, bang,
driving nails into the hard flesh of the tree.
The congregation wriggled at each blow.
My aunt undid the two top buttons of her blouse.
My uncle dribbled into the collection plate.

On either side I felt them squeeze me.
My heart went thump, thump, thump
and my hair crackled and flashed.
I was called the holy child of Ardnamurchan.
All through the service what big hands they had!

That old Devil is coming for me
across the fields I know.
'Little children!' he calls. 'Little children!
Is you there?'
He is black
from his rolling eyes to the size of his thing
and more terrible.
He grins and licks his nigger chops.
Outside the church the sea goes boom, boom, boom.

SEA AND SKY

Sea and sky. Earthbound as I am
I've never yet been able to decide
which one I like best. I'd live,
I think, for preference on the sea.
I'd farm there a more fruitful soil
than what surrounds me here.
I'd be a connoisseur of gulls
and every day I'd open a new horizon.

I'd choose the sky for burial
though, if such were possible.
I'd have mountains at my head and feet.
When Gabriel blew his trumpet I'd arrive
before God's kindness became strained.
The clouds would ease my bones
more than the hard rocks of Ardnamurchan.
Not worms would feed on me but larks.

Our mountains are indifferent to it.
They go right through the earth
and are riveted on the other side.
Such weather merely bounces off them,
blunting itself on their hunched backs.

It's another story at this level.
Streams out of control career downhill.
Fields drum and buckle, tearing loose
from their fenceposts. My house is adrift
in the garden, battering against the wall.

I, too, tilt with the landscape.
My mind is not on gimballs.
I'd pray if there were anyone to pray to.
I'm sure that God has stuffed his ears
with bits of cloud to drown the noise.

My salvation must be here if anywhere.
I have fired my last flare.
All I can do now is hold on.
Great seas come rolling in from space.
The world rocks at its anchor.

THOUGHTS AFTER RAIN

I

Living in rain, I'd say, would take great skill.
Even just walking in it, for a start,
what with one's upturned face and trying to
avoid the gaps, is pretty much of an art.

But walking in all this mud is a vocation.
My feet are guided less by sight than sound.
I pick up acres at each step and place
them down elsewhere. I pollinate the ground.

All has to be re-made, re-used. I work
on out-at-elbow streams, their sleeves grown tight.
I groom bedraggled grass and plate the hills
and set pools everywhere to catch the light.

And I've improved our brook: once slug-a-bed
and small and pale, now quick and huge and brown;
once parasitic merely on the eyes
and now a shield between us and the town.

The chaos falls on me. It's my job to
re-form a mass or re-define a border.
I've simply had a metaphor thrust at me
and been told to put the disarray in order.

II

I was condemned once to a desert life
in India. I was a prisoner of the sun.

My ear turned simple, seeming never to
have heard a lake lap or a river run.

It was the first time ever I regretted
my contact with the surface of the world.
I feared to catch up on my sleep by day
lest I should lie down flat and wake up curled.

I sleep less now. I note the greenness peeling
from the fields, uncovering bare skin,
the stink of necromancy in the air
and comforters grown fat and poets grown thin.

Cherish the rain! Diviners multiply,
yet everywhere the cry goes up for more.
The hazel won't be thwarted; it will dip
to blood at last. There are dry days in store.

EAGLES

When it was a poor parish
that didn't have its Giant,
pissing rivers, orbiting boulders,
suffocating villages
each time he drew a breath,

there were eagles here, real ones,
evading easily those clumsy arms,
duelling with wolves, kidnapping babies,
darkening the sky
while going about their proper business.

Their wings could power a windmill.
Their talons were like steel cages.
They were royal creatures Fingal brought
from Ireland.
Three of their eggs made a dozen.

An eagle of that breed once, for a joke,
picked up a stunted Highlander
and flew him south, witless from the journey
but fertile still.
Hence your race of Lowland Scots.

And that's the way I like my eagles.
I wouldn't give you tuppence for this lot.
Scaled-down usurpers. Sparrow-hawks.
Mini-birds.
We get the sort of eagles we deserve.

HEN DYING

The old grey hen is dying
who once was so cheeky.
For ten years or more
I've not been able to leave the house
without her begging bowl
being thrust in front of me.
You have to be in the mood for hens.
Some days I had my heart set on people.

She's learning now about queues and things
and how the spring sunshine
rests more heavily on some hens
than on others.
She sits by herself over near the byre.
Her head's pulled in like a tortoise's.
Her eyelids are half drawn-down.

The other hens have cast her out.
They batter her with their beaks
whenever they come across her.
Most of them are her daughters.
Hens are inhuman.

She doesn't visit the feed any more.
I lay some grain in front of her
whenever I come across her.
She rummages through her mind,
slowly remembering how to eat.

One of these days she'll fall over.
I'll make a coffin from a shoebox for her
and tie it with a piece of ribbon.
I'll bury her in a corner of the stackyard
between two stooks of corn.

That's holy ground to hens and crofters.
The earth is dry and sandy there
and the worm count is as low
as any place in Ardnamurchan.
For a week or two I'll miss her.

Crow, crow, crow. Was here on the first day.
Flew around, waiting for the crust to cool.
Did not evolve. Started off this way.

Gets fatter as the world gets leaner.
Eats carrion, adders, frogs, what have you.
A sort of airborne vacuum-cleaner.

Knocks limpets off rocks. Cracks
lobster claws. Bill is the hardest substance known.
You could use a dead crow for a pickaxe.

Played truant when they gave out pity.
Takes the eyes from a sheep in labour.
Sober-suited. Would do well in the City.

Roars with laughter at a snare. Knows a trick
worth two of that. Won't come near an armed man.
Can tell a shotgun from a walking-stick.

Our parish records list one ancient kill,
staked down at a crossroads late at night.
A neighbour keeps a feather as an heirloom still.

OUR BULL

He has the slimmest hips
and the most massive shoulders.
Viewed from the front
he's the width of a whole field.

His kingdom is red-rimmed.
Everything that moves in it he stops.
Everything that's stopped he moves.

Pressure builds up in him periodically.
His sides heave and quiver.
Jets of steam gush from his nostrils.
One more pound per square inch
and he'd explode.

Even at rest in the long grass
he's still a metaphor for danger:
the round black hump of his back,
horn tips rising over it,
bobs menacingly in the green swell.

Standing he dominates the landscape.
Tourists sweat their way past him
at fifty yards or more,
feeling with outstretched toes
for the next foothold.
The women say nothing;
a tendency to dawdle
when almost safe
reveals the difference
between the fear they'd own to
and the one they hide.

No blame to them.
He moves from legend to reality with ease
and brings the best part of his story with him.
His bellowing is preliminary only. He delivers.

Yet he will follow a cow
about to come in heat
so modestly he seems to shrink.
He accepts her insults meekly
and keeps his weapon sheathed.
One thrust through the vitals pays for all.

Or in a randy mood, no cows available,
he'll stab the air, semen dripping from him

in the ambiguous prodigality of nature.
Our bull is state-owned
and will be salvaged by and by.
Someone in an office somewhere
charts his progress.
Calf production is plotted against time
and the curve goes down.

I was given once
the chance to watch a bull,
his services all done,
being poleaxed in a slaughterhouse.
He died so quickly and so heavily
I trembled.
Before my heart
had ceased to register the shock
he was chained and swung,
a bucket hung from his horns
and his throat tapped.

TALLYMAN

It must be easily
the hottest day so far this year.
Along the crest of the Glendryan Hills
the grass snaps under my feet.
If it were dark the rocks would glow.

I see the flies and hear them
before I see the sheep they quarrel over.
A cloud of bluebottles
thick enough to cast a shadow.
When she moves off at my approach
they rev up and follow.

Maggots, of course. You could scoop them
off her back in handfuls.
Small carnivorous worms with non-stop appetites,
they worry her to death.
The flies wait for the bones.

Sheep die unnoticed as a rule.
I was lucky to come across this one.
They go apart when their time comes
but without knowing why. They die instinctively.

I fan myself with my notebook.
It was cooler after all at sea level.
A stray bluebottle
follows me persistently all the way down.

I HATE MIDSUMMER IN THE NORTH

I hate midsummer in the north.
There's no night to speak of,
just day in and day in
with maybe a slight hesitancy
about two o'clock in the morning.

The sun's at work continually,
zooming in from some part of the sky,
at some angle or another. In time
it penetrates the thickest skull. In time
it levers up the most forbidding brow.

Light pours down. It makes things clear.
I see there's only one world
after all, and it's a hot one
and a bright one. My hayfield
curls up at the corners. My lips, too.

While the days swagger, elbow one another,
I wait, with what sadness I can muster.
This white weather doesn't suit me,
I think. I get fatter all the time.
For weeks I live off my stored darkness.

JAMES MACKENZIE

He shambles, open-flyed but harmless, three weeks
out of four, does simple jobs for tips,
could point the churchyard where the headstones tell
how much inbreeding dribbles from his lips.

But each waxed moon his manhood swells, pretending to
what's unobtainable. His vision frames
a world subdued to his great rise and thrust.
All flesh he runs, runs through flames.

Lashed to a bedtop at the peak, leathered
and buckled, his ape arms cord and strain.
His fingers close on nothing more than air.
His running feet drum on the counterpane.

To be tied then is insupportable.
His lungs focus his rage. Frustration's self
he drives his bellows through the matchwood house
till the shocked dishes tremble on the shelf.

There's no one can survive within his room.
A deaf man once who thought to beat that cry
was frozen on the spot till the fit was past,
shafted and held on his red murderous eye.

THREE-LEGGED FROG

A frog emerges from the fallen hay
that lies beneath my scythe,
trailing its right hind-leg behind it,
joined now only by a strip of skin.

What must it be like
to be without a limb?

I balance experimentally on one foot.
The frog lurches towards a ditch,
its severed member banging
uselessly against its body,
a traveller with an empty suitcase.

THE OLD DOG

Useless.
Our shouts bounce off him.
His eyes, each pasted over
with cataract,
tilt upwards
to the surreptitious claps
that span his days.
The furniture,
he finds,
is still predictable;
the people never were.
Inevitably
we get under his feet.
We curse him and keep him.

DEATH OF AN OLD WOMAN

She lived too much alone to be aware of it,
in a cottage on a stretch of moor,
built before the distant road was built
and shunned by everything built since.
Her croft had faded through the years
for lack of drainage and proper food,
bled of its green until the eye
could hardly tell where it began or ended.
Her house had a hole in the thatch
to let the smoke out—when there was any—
and the rain in, and three small openings
in the walls, two for light and one for charity,
and all about the size she was accustomed to.
The man who found her dead was drawn
in that direction by the movement.
That was the door of her empty henhouse
flapping in the wind, a nerve continuing to twitch.
She herself was lying in her bed,
causing a slight ripple in the blankets.
She had an English Bible in her hands,
upside down. The doctor who examined her
stated that her mouth was full of raw potato.

DEATH OF A HIND

The hind, knocked sprawling by my shot,
rises and weaves about the clearing
like a stage drunk going round a lamppost.
But when I arrive, panting, at her side,
she marshals her straying legs and lines
them up beneath her in a last-ditch effort
at sobriety of direction. It's no use.
Some instincts points her at the fleeing herd
but only her will gallops. While I sweat,
curse and tear at the jammed spent cartridge
she waits, patient now, wielding her dignity.
I clear the jam at last. My bullet,
sawn off at the tip, punches into her.
It unclenches its fist inside her heart.

RAMS

Their horns are pure baroque,
as thick at the root as a man's wrist.
They have golden eyes and Roman noses.
All the ewes love them.

They are well-equipped to love back.
In their prime they balance;
the sex at one end of their bodies
equalling the right to use it at the other.

When two of them come face to face
in the mating season
a spark jumps the gap.
Their heads drive forward like cannon balls.
Solid granite hills splinter into echoes.

They never wrestle, as stags and bulls do.
They slug it out. The hardest puncher wins.
Sometimes they back up so far for a blow
they lose sight of one another
and just start grazing.

They are infinitely and indefatigably stupid.
You can rescue the same one
from the same bramble bush
fifty times.
Such a massive casing to guard such a tiny brain
—as if Fort Knox were built to house a single penny!

But year by year those horns add growth.
The sex is outstripped in the end;
the balance tilts in the direction of the head.

I found a ram dead once.
It was trapped by the forefeet
in the dark waters of a peatbog,
drowned before help could arrive
by the sheer weight of its skull.
Maiden ewes were grazing near it,
immune to its clangorous lust.
It knelt on the bank, hunched over its own image,
its great head buried in the great head facing it.
Its horns, going forward in the old way,
had battered through at last to the other side.

When I look out at the stunted hay,
by harvest time no closer to the sun
than what it was in April,
not taking from this land so much as giving to it,
my mind most dwells on Hugh Maclean,
who was, like me, tutor to three poor acres.
His beasts went about in their bones,
as mine go about,
and so unschooled and rude his winters came
and never left till everything was eaten.
One evening, as he thought of it, his learning failed.
The clock was drumming on the mantelpiece
and the first gale of the season
had just edged beneath his door
and drawn itself up to its full height.
'I was not actually born bitter,' he said,
'but even as a child I was observant.
And those are two sounds
I have been listening to for long enough.'
It happened that he owned a shotgun
but had only one cartridge to his name.
When daylight came he went out to his field,
wedged the gun inside a crevice,
and pulled the trigger with a piece of string.
The shot took him low in the body
and folded him,
no more than half dead at the most
and with the gaining of the other half
looking like a long and painful business.
His daughter had come running from the house.
'Club me with the butt,' he ordered her.

'Strike as hard as you can and then go home.
Give me till tomorrow morning.'
'I will neither help you nor hinder you,'
she answered, 'and I will stay with you.'
He remembered that the river ran its course
a quarter of a mile away and crawled towards it,
she following him at a distance,
walking to one side of the blood.
'It was a long journey,'
was all she ever said of it in later life.
On the bank he stripped somehow
and somehow waded in waist-deep,
expecting that the water would soak up the blood.
But he'd forgotten one thing
—our river rises among mountains
where the snow never sets
and as it goes along it recollects its source.
Only pebbles thrive in it
and cold-blooded water-weeds.
The chill of it cauterised his wounds.
When he looked down at his belly
he saw a dozen tiny mouths,
all with thin lips primly clamped together.
'On any other day,' he said to them,
'the wind would have prised you open.'
Still in midstream he pleaded
with the watching girl to fetch a knife,
met the same refusal,
and climbed out himself a moment
to scour the field for a sharp-bladed stone.
One came to his hand.
The river sucked away his blood then
and when it fell below the level of his heart
he died.

His daughter lived to be an old woman.
I can just remember her.
Every year upon the anniversary
a neighbour was elected to present her with a knife.
She had scores of them at last but no money.
That was cruel!
God send me such a loving child!
The field where once her passion flowered
is given over now to reeds.
No use to man or beast
and therefore flourishing.
I don't know of any other place,
not even the Great Bog of Glendryan,
where they grow so tall and so broad.

VIEW FROM MY WINDOW

The scourge of wind first, to flay
the last layer of vegetation from the hills,
then this deluge, obliterating wind and hills,
the eye going out from the ark and returning.

A bleak, inhuman, fearful landscape:
something to roll up and stow in my mind
against those odd moments of happiness.

FISHING

We fish
in a sea worn smooth by last week's gales,
so flat and glassy
that if you breathed on it, it would mist.
There's no depth to it.
When I lean over the side
someone drops a weighted hook towards me.
Fish should come
through the hole he makes in my skull
but none do.
In the bottom of the boat
there lies just one small mackerel,
caught hours ago,
its colours dulled by its long immersion.

My father leans back on the oars;
a touch now and again is all he needs
to keep us stem first to the tide.
His left hand knows what his right is doing.
'When I was young,' he says, 'it was worthwhile.'
He casts his mind back into the past
and fish after fish rises to the kill.
The deeper he goes the bigger they get.
When he was a boy
they were as tall almost as himself.
'It was before your time,' he says.
'It was before the trawlers came.'

Yes. I know about the trawlers.
I pretend to be examining my coat sleeve
but am really looking at my watch.

'There will be time,' it says, 'before your time'
but when I breathe on it, it mists.
A catspaw dances across the water.
The Atlantic opens one eye, then goes back to sleep.

THE PEACEABLE KINGDOM

The Adder

Guardian of the wild places is the adder.
That long footprint is a boundary.

There must be fear beyond delight
or else delight would never end.
Patrick drove the adders out of Ireland,
as Plato drove the poets from Greece,
and two by two his flock was lost to him
among the unpoliced grass.
But here he never came
and no one's footsteps left the road.

'Adders' was a word we never used
when I was young.
We called them serpents
as our elders taught us,
and all my childhood venom reigned
for there's no antidote to language.

The Ant

I do not like ants or admire them.
It isn't skill that crams those chambers
but content,
a perfect knowledge of the body's joints
and how the mind works,
submission to God's rules for ants.

The tiger misses one in every twenty hinds
and the falcon has to climb laboriously up again
but who ever saw an unsuccessful ant?

I held my hands down in a nest
when I was small,
because I wanted to,
and ran home gloved with ants.
My father plunged my hands in scalding water,
a split second only,
and the gloves peeled perfectly off.

But out there in the fields
there lie the fatherless dead,
gaping, gaping;
many of them, it's true,
but the ants are manier still.

The Buzzard

The buzzard turns a circle in the sky,
making its ends meet.
When it completes the figure
a round blue segment drops out of the air,
leaving a black hole
through which the souls of many little birds
fly up to heaven.

The Cormorant

It's a fish-processing factory,
a headlong appetite.
The gobbling gull's a dilettante in comparison.

It shuttles between roosting rock
and feeding ground,
threaded on the straight line of its gut,
ignorant of the blue miles stacked above it.

If you disturb a cormorant
it doesn't fly, it dives.
It takes the path of least resistance,
becomes the feathered eel
that it's evolving toward
and comes up in another part of the ocean.

The Crow

The first crow that I remember
occurred when I was eight or nine.
It flew above me,
slantwise across the sky.
It called three times,
in a harsh loud voice:
'God! God! God!'

The Cuckoo

We hear according to our need.
No doubt this bird existed
when I was a boy
but what I listened to was earth and sea.
There was enough of sadness
for my young requirements
in universal things.

I have a man's appetite now,
a taste for specificity,
and all day long
my ears are tuned to 'Cuckoo! Cuckoo!'
that lancing shout
in two syllables, repeated:
up, down; in, out.

The Dog

This creature came to guard our flocks
and stayed to foul our minds.
I would not have a dog
except at need
to throw a living lasso
round a sheep.
My father owns a collie bitch
and she adores me.
When we meet
I feel the poet in me subsiding,
the master coming out.

A tourist I saw once
was coming down our road,
making his way in the world
behind a huge Alsatian dog.
A steel chain linked the two of them.
Maleness flowed along it from dog to man.

The Fox

One clear morning after weeks of rain
I went into the world
to see who else had clung to it.

47

The water lapped around the hills
and halfway up the highest one
I saw a fox,
a bit bedraggled, yes,
but you could tell
he'd been to a good school.
The sun shone for him.
He was stopped
at the junction of two trails,
turning over a heap of scents
in search of a bargain.

I remember as clearly as a dream
the year of the foxes,
how they flourished,
how pairs grew into families
and families to tribes
and tribes to armies,
how, maddened by success,
they came roaring through our villages,
shoulder to shoulder and rooftop thick,
twisting and leaping,
consuming everything,
one fox almost,
a red torrent.

We crouched naked at the water's edge
and shivering.
There was only west to go.
We crowded onto a piece of wood
until we blackened it
and were pushed out into the water,
the fox getting rid of its fleas.

The Peregrine

His working eye has seen me
long before my leisure one sees him.
He straddles acres, treading air,
and sifts the turning world below
through meshes beetle-fine.

Computerised by evolution
he calculates the angle of the sun and wind
and the flight-path of a pigeon.
He adds them up
and finds the answer underneath.

Man sows his fields with poison now
and death works up the scale as well as down.
It isn't prey
this falcon bears so lightly off
but a Trojan Horse.

The Seal

The seal lounges in the surf,
stuffing fish into its mouth with both hands,
balancing the world on the end of its nose.
Only human music pierces its content
and makes it leg it up the beach,
so in reverse
those men who hear it singing
weep and find the logic of their salty tears
drives them into the surf.

When all the seals are landsmen
and all the landsmen seals
then, say our Highland legends,
the sky will darken
and judgement begin to fall

The Shark

Sharks, like snakes, are imprinted on our genes:
the directions read 'Thrill!'

Other harmless creatures ape the shark:
the so-called basking-shark, for instance.
That's known as protective mimicry.
It works.
The textbooks differentiate; the genes don't.

The closer to a shark you get
the bigger it becomes.
And that's known as cowardice.
I got very close to one one day
when I was fishing from a boat off Ardnamurchan.
It overtook me
where I hung above a mackerel swarm,
forcing me to back off to make room.
The day by luck was calm enough
for me to demonstrate my monarchism.
I stood between the thwarts and cheered
as foot by foot the long procession passed me.

The Wolf

Man is a man to wolf.
Because it would not lower its belly
to the dust
this creature had to be destroyed.

So 'bang' we went and 'bang' and 'bang'
till savagery faded from our hills
and every costermonger was clad in wolfskin.

Yet in a few places wolves linger still,
protected by wise shepherds
and waiting for an end to dog days.

The Worm

Worms have a nose for beauty.
Where they most breed and haunt
I have observed the skin is delicate.

I found them underneath
the most voluptuous breast
and where the silk hair parts the fingers.
And that was why I turned aside.
Well, a man would have to be made of iron.

They say old age brings friendship
between worm and man.
I'll prove that false.
Never across my threshold
by connivance or consent
shall this creature pass.

I want to die
curled up in a corner
with my teeth bared.

Bury me above the ground, in bronze.
Let my inscription read:
this man was singular and true;
he was not reconciled to the worm.

HEDGEHOGS AND GEESE

Hedgehogs undermine the winter.
Shrouded in old leaves
they let the edges of their bodies die.
They retreat into their own hearts.

Geese, too, retreat before the ice
but south instead of under.
They burrow with their wings.
Down the long tunnels of the skies
they hurtle, talking to themselves,
a conversation encoded by the wind
and by their unimaginable history.
At zero latitude they nod.
They pull the equator over their heads
and go to sleep.

Each year I study these alternatives,
pursuing kinship in a hardening world.
My eyes lift to the geese at first,
a moment lured by height
and uncorrupted space
—one's fill of distances!
But that's the vision unbraced by the will
or the spirit premature as usual.
At heart no flyer
I bristle timidly when touched.
When the ice comes I retreat beneath it.
I choose at last hedgehogs.

WAITING-DAYS

A waiting-day is pale and still, a dead day
in the middle of the living season,
a day on which you stop from time to time
to listen but for no apparent reason.

And in between your spells of listening
you wait, for all must give that day its due
and, crippled or alone or both, you know
the loved and nimble wait as well as you.

Even the creatures wait, being troubled by
a something closer to the nape than fear.
But what this waiting grows to I have
never yet found out, though I've come near:

I drove in for provisions once along
our only road and never left its crown,
yet managed to slip sideways as I travelled
and came at journey's end to a strange town.

A pipe and slippers sort of town it was,
one eye on God, the other on the books,
but empty, empty; half-eaten meals
on tables but no diners and no cooks.

And there were children there who'd left their shouts
behind, so quickly had they gone from play,
and empty buildings still warm to the touch
and empty streets that pointed all one way.

And faintly from some distant square,
as I stood waiting in that town,
I heard a drum begin to gather speed
and heard, too, a great axe come down.

THE BEACH IN WINTER

Where every yard of ground was civilised
by deckchairs, there's nothing now
to cushion me from metaphor.
A gull, at my approach, hurls itself
into the wind and is knocked sideways
by the impact. In the shallows,
in the backwash of each wave,
long arms of tangle heave above the surface,
signal once or twice and disappear.
And higher up the beach I note
a certain kind of wading bird
that runs among the debris,
scavenging the outgoing tide,
methodically turning over small stones.

AMONG OURSELVES

Among ourselves we rarely speak;
our tongues are thick with custom.
Inside our house, at this time of the year,
there's only the ticking of the clock
and the click of my mother's needles
as she knits herself away from where
she cast on. My father's pages rustle.
He makes himself a nest of newspaper.
I sit in a corner, smoking. Every time
I draw on my cigarette I hear
the tiny hiss of tobacco becoming ash.

HOME THOUGHTS FROM HOME

No doubt I'm spoiled. One's soon accustomed to
being plied with spoonfuls of the best of jam.
It's only when at home that I forgo
the luxury of knowing who I am.

And to decide with some exactness what
my status is would be a lifetime's labour,
though not perhaps of love. I am not brother
to my brothers quite, more next-door neighbour.

My parents, too, have faded from my sight,
lost in a wondering air of 'Well, I never!'
There's no way back. I've lost the knack of them.
I've been away too long and grown too clever.

Well, I suppose each rescues what he needs
from time and mounts it under pin and label.
It's something, that. But oh! those glances
that avoid my glance, that politesse at table.

If you're a peasant who writes poetry
and bear the stamp of it on all you say
your family are those you visit most
and home is how they live when you're away.

PRAYER GOING DOWNHILL

I see the old poet in *The Times* today,
his new allegiance stressed,
and ladies taking tea with him,
not one of them undressed;

participant in hollow rites
that once he would have mocked;
surrounded by adoring flesh,
his little finger cocked.

Entombed in admiration thus
he's dead before his time;
Lord, give me praise but let me have
enough neglect to rhyme.

Let all my speech be common speech
and linger in the mouth;
preserve for me my mug and keep
the teacups in the south.

Let my concern for being clean
never do me hurt.
Sterile artist, sterile art;
now, God, stand up for dirt!

You poured a deal of gentleness
and neatness into my span.
Now, if You love me, let me be
a fierce unkempt old man.

CHURCH AND CHILD

The church I went to as a boy was many
hundred cubits long and many broad and tall.
It was hewn in one piece from the solid rock
and carpeted with winter wall to wall.

It had no stained glass to inflame the soul
and lipsticked girls were scrubbed and then put out.
It was by northern law itself unheated, since
whatever kindled warmth might kindle doubt.

It had hard oak for your back and small windows
too high to let you see how comfortably sat God.
It was surrounded by the dead in thickening rows
whom I thought but ill-secured beneath their sod.

It stood aloft. You had to push your faith up to it
as Sisyphus pushed his boulder up the slope.
Yet, not to be a churchgoer in that age and place
—ah, you might as well be English or the Pope!

It had an air of needing not to move but once,
when ill, I prayed God shutter all our house
lest I should see the church come down the hill
for me, the mousetrap coming for the mouse.

Yet those were the days! And, oh, the easy way
with tears I had when I was six or seven!
The child has taken on the outline of
a man now and the church has gone to heaven.

WHAT IT COSTS

When first I started trafficking for poems
how unconcernedly I played my part!
I traded, drop by drop, my blood and smiled
to think of the red gallons in my heart.

How could I guess that though my trading soon
produced too much of worth to let me quit
a day would come when I would fear and hate
the pain and the indignity of it?

TWO BY ONE

Town birds are mated in the spring and tell
of it and the branched stags in autumn shout.
Loudness and twoness blend at all times
and everywhere to mock the ones without.

Man also duplicates, each pleased to have
the necessary other by his side.
Those unconnected find the passing years
but mark the slow erosion of their pride.

It is the mean shifts forced on the unpaired
that kill. My whole half-life I have been one
who in the country stands beside his door
at dusk to watch the village lamps come on,

and waits as long as one is still unlit
and opportunity for hurt remains
or, aimless haunter of a city station,
convincingly inquires about late trains.

How comforting are boundaries! They define things.
Day after day I'm drawn to this clifftop. I seek
that reassurance, though I get less of it each time

or say I need more of the edge to produce it.
Today I jut my ten toes out over the Atlantic
where it most is. Five hundred feet below me fish swim.

Strange! I fear heights as I fear my own company
yet here I stand and am mocked by seagulls
whose lightness overtook them a billion years ago.

Think then what it must be like to go down from here,
through the astonished birds and the water
to a new country, for visa your pockets full of stones.

You live your life again, they say, before you drown.
But in reverse, I think. The years erase themselves
and the anguish with them. Your birth ends everything.

Down you go, with the pressure rising to meet you;
down to a point of balance. You drift in equilibrium then,
your legs forever dangling, like a foetus in a jar.

Or you come back to the sun after many days,
to loll and sidle on the surface, unsinkable
and vast, your tongue stuck out at the world.

But coming back's the rub, for it's a new death
you resurrect to, a more thoroughgoing one,
with all your blubbery secrets yielded up.

The seagulls call and call in their unearthly voices.
How many cliffs would have to come and go to hang me
in their sky? But that's a different sort of dead end.

At least they quicken to no impulse, suffer no regret.
I think that always between the trigger and the flesh
there stands a huge but penetrable 'No!'

I do not wish to take that step. Not ever!
Why then do I loiter on this high threshold
till room beyond and room behind darken into one?

ENVOY

On Meall nan Con, the Peak of the Dogs,
two skeletons of stags lie head to head,
both royals, their antlers laced together.

I watched the fight that led to this
and watched without complaint
the long death that followed it.

A hummel served the hinds that year
whose strength was all between his legs,
not growing from his skull in antique patterns.

It is with diffidence I note their struggle.
A still more ancient craft they studied,
each bonded to the master opposite.

The deer is noble, a Roman animal.
I remember how the grass was trampled
and how finally they loved each other.